IMAGES
OF GOD

10 STUDIES FOR INDIVIDUALS OR GROUPS

Dale & Sandy Larsen

With Notes for Leaders

IVP Connect

An imprint of InterVarsity Press
Downers Grove, Illinois

InterVarsity Press
P.O. Box 1400, Downers Grove, IL 60515-1426
World Wide Web: www.ivpress.com
E-mail: email@ivpress.com

InterVarsity Press® is the book-publishing division of InterVarsity Christian Fellowship/USA®, a movement of students and faculty active on campus at hundreds of universities, colleges and schools of nursing in the United States of America, and a member movement of the International Fellowship of Evangelical Students. For information about local and regional activities, write Public Relations Dept., InterVarsity Christian Fellowship/USA, 6400 Schroeder Rd., P.O. Box 7895, Madison, WI 53707-7895, or visit the IVCF website at <www.intervarsity.org>.

LifeGuide® is a registered trademark of InterVarsity Christian Fellowship.

Cover image: Dennis Flaherty

ISBN 978-0-8308-3001-5

Printed in the United States of America ∞

P   20   19   18   17   16   15   14   13   12   11   10   9   8

Y   24   23   22   21   20   19   18   17   16   15   14

Contents

Getting the Most Out of
Images of God

Recently in a Bible study group we were asked this question: "What was your earliest idea of God?"

The group members' answers varied widely: a picture of Jesus, a great puffy cloud, an old man on a throne, a fiery sunset, a robed minister behind the pulpit. Everyone in the group agreed that our childhood ideas of God were inadequate. Yet it was also obvious that, for all of us, our early images were significant and powerful. We could not forget them. Decades later they we still with us.

Those childhood images of deity, insufficient as they were, had given us a mental hook on which to hang the name "God." They had lent some tangible shape and form to a Person who was so mysterious, so different from us, that otherwise we could hardly think of him at all.

When we study Scripture, we discover that thinking of God in earthly terms is not so childish after all. The Holy Spirit led the writers of Scripture to use poetic language and compare the Lord to all sorts of ordinary things on earth. We can call these word pictures "images of God" because they help us to mentally see the unseeable, the "King of kings and Lord of lords, who alone is immortal and who lives in unapproachable light, whom no one has seen or can see" (1 Timothy 6:15-16).

Among the many images of God in the Bible, we have chosen ten for this study guide. Some are from nature, some from the world of work, some from family or social roles. (We will deal with images which are specific to Jesus Christ and the Holy Spirit in the LifeGuides *Images of Jesus* and *Images of the Holy Spirit*.)

As we study each of these scriptural word pictures of God, our interest is not simply to indulge in poetic picture-making. We want to focus on *our relationship to the reality behind the image.* We may gaze at a rock fortress in the middle of a field and admire its strength, but it does us no good unless we take refuge in it. We may stand in awe of a warrior's power, but we must get involved in his battles. We may praise the fairness of a judge, but the time comes when we must stand before him ourselves. We may admire the potter's handiwork, but then we discover that *we* are the clay he is trying to mold.

At the conclusion of each study you will find three extra features:

- Guidance for prayer. Feel free to use these ideas whether you are studying in a group or individually.

- A "Now or Later" section. This includes suggestions for further study and ways to confirm the lesson and apply it to everyday life.

- A list of hymns based on the scriptural image. Many hymns have been inspired by the rich poetic imagery of the Bible. You may sing one or more of them, or simply read the words. The lists are not exhaustive! You will probably recall other hymns or choruses based on each image.

The more we studied the biblical images of God, the more we stood in awe of both God's mystery and his humility. He allows us to think of him in the most earthly terms, so we can better understand the One who is ultimately beyond our understanding. May God lead you to know him better through these inspired word portraits of himself.

Suggestions for Individual Study

1. As you begin each study, pray that God will speak to you through his Word.

2. Read the introduction to the study and respond to the personal reflection question or exercise. This is designed to help you focus on God and on the theme of the study.

3. Each study deals with a particular passage—so that you can delve into the author's meaning in that context. Read and reread the passage to be studied. The questions are written using the language of the New International Version, so you may wish to use that version of the Bible. The New Revised Standard Version is also recommended.

4. This is an inductive Bible study, designed to help you discover for yourself what Scripture is saying. The study includes three types of questions. *Observation* questions ask about the basic facts: who, what, when, where and how. *Interpretation* questions delve into the meaning of the passage. *Application* questions help you discover the implications of the text for growing in Christ. These three keys unlock the treasures of Scripture.

Write your answers to the questions in the spaces provided or in a personal journal. Writing can bring clarity and deeper understanding of yourself and of God's Word.

5. It might be good to have a Bible dictionary handy. Use it to look up any unfamiliar words, names or places.

6. Use the prayer suggestion to guide you in thanking God for what you have learned and to pray about the applications that have come to mind.

7. You may want to go on to the suggestion under "Now or Later," or you may want to use that idea for your next study.

Suggestions for Members of a Group Study

1. Come to the study prepared. Follow the suggestions for individual study mentioned above. You will find that careful preparation will greatly enrich your time spent in group discussion.

2. Be willing to participate in the discussion. The leader of your group will not be lecturing. Instead, he or she will be encouraging the members of the group to discuss what they have learned. The leader will be asking the questions that are found in this guide.

3. Stick to the topic being discussed. Your answers should be based on the verses which are the focus of the discussion and not on outside authorities such as commentaries or speakers. These studies focus on a particular passage of Scripture. Only rarely should you refer to other portions of the Bible. This allows for everyone to participate in in-depth study on equal ground.

4. Be sensitive to the other members of the group. Listen attentively when they describe what they have learned. You may be surprised by their insights! Each question assumes a variety of answers. Many questions do not have "right" answers, particularly questions that aim at meaning or application. Instead the questions push us to explore the passage more thoroughly.

When possible, link what you say to the comments of others. Also, be affirming whenever you can. This will encourage some of the more hesitant members of the group to participate.

5. Be careful not to dominate the discussion. We are sometimes so eager to express our thoughts that we leave too little opportunity for others to respond. By all means participate! But allow others to also.

6. Expect God to teach you through the passage being discussed and through the other members of the group. Pray that you will have an enjoyable and profitable time together, but also that as a result of the study you will find ways that you can take action individually and/or as a group.

7. Remember that anything said in the group is considered confidential and should not be discussed outside the group unless specific permission is given to do so.

8. If you are the group leader, you will find additional suggestions at the back of the guide.

1

Rock

In Harvey Mackay's book about business success, *Swim With the Sharks Without Being Eaten Alive,* one chapter is headed, "There's a place in the world for anyone in the world who says, 'I'll take care of it.'" Mackay says when your boss hands you a job, no matter how tedious or ridiculous it is, you should immediately respond "I'll take care of it." It's an easy promise to make but not so easy to carry out consistently. Our good intentions get sidetracked. We get busy; other things seem more urgent or more interesting; we forget our promises.

In an insecure world, David found God to be consistent and dependable. No matter what the problem, as long as David depended on God, God would take care of it. And God has not changed. As he was a rock and fortress for David, we can trust him to be a rock and fortress for us.

GROUP DISCUSSION. When you tackle a group project, how does it affect your attitude if the leadership is dependable? undependable?

PERSONAL REFLECTION. Would you call yourself a dependable person? In what areas would you like to be more dependable?

Many of David's psalms rose from urgent need, when he prayed desperately for God's help. In the case of Psalm 31 we are not told what sort of trouble David faced. Perhaps we are left in the dark so we can freely apply his words to troubles of our own. *Read Psalm 31:1-8.*

1. In your own words, what did David expect from God?

2. From what David wrote here, why do you think he was so confident in his expectations?

3. As you were reading through this passage, what problems of your own (solved or unsolved) came to your mind?

4. In the landscape of Palestine, David must have found many rocky places to hide from his enemies. Why is it significant that David says God *is* his rock, fortress and refuge (vv. 2-4) rather than that God *provides* those things?

5. How had the Lord proved himself dependable for David (vv. 6-8)?

6. What makes a rocky place a good refuge as opposed to other places?

7. What are some undependable fortresses people seek for security?

8. What is one fortress you have tried and found undependable?

9. How have you found God to be a rock of refuge and a fortress? Think of ways he has been a spiritual as well as a physical fortress.

10. On the cross just before he died, Jesus quoted part of verse 5: "Into your hands I commit my spirit" (Luke 23:46), prefacing it with "Father." How does knowing that affect your view of this psalm?

11. In contrast to the rocklike qualities of God, how does David portray himself throughout this passage?

12. Suppose a critic said, "The writer of this psalm was a coward. He would show more courage if he faced his enemies instead of fleeing to a fortress." How would you answer that objection?

13. In what part(s) of life are you tempted to take unwise risks in the face of spiritual danger, either deliberately or by ignoring the hazards?

14. With God's help, how will you change your attitudes or behavior to take shelter in the Lord, your rock of refuge?

Thank the Lord that he is absolutely dependable. Pray for wisdom to see and avoid spiritual dangers. Pray also for the wisdom to know when physical hazard is God's choice for you and when it is only foolishness.

Now or Later

- Get the fuller story of David's prayer by studying the rest of Psalm 31.
- Study two other psalms in which God is called a rock or a fortress: Psalm 18 and Psalm 91.
- In a Bible handbook or other reference book, read about the geology of Palestine, particularly about rocky hills used as fortresses.
- Write about a time when the Lord protected you (physically or spiritually) but you did not realize it until later.

Suggested hymns to read or sing
How Firm a Foundation
A Mighty Fortress Is Our God
The Solid Rock (My Hope Is Built on Nothing Less)
Rock of Ages
O Safe to the Rock That Is Higher Than I

2

Warrior

Exodus 15:1-18

When someone gets into a bad situation and wants a rescuer to magically appear, we say the person is looking for a "knight in shining armor." We mean that the person should stop daydreaming about rescue and get to work to improve the situation.

In history, knights were more than daydreams. They were real warriors who fought real battles. When we are defeated by life or by our own failings, we need a warrior to show up and fight our battles for us. That's when we want God the all-powerful Warrior on our side— or rather, we want to make sure we are on *his* side!

GROUP DISCUSSION. What are some of the most exhausting battles of the Christian life?

PERSONAL REFLECTION. What are the qualities of a good soldier?

The Israelite people were slaves in Egypt until Moses, who was sent and empowered by God, rallied them and led them out. Then the Egyptian pharaoh changed his mind about letting them go and came after them. Trapped on the shore of the Red Sea, Israel cried out to God, and the water parted so they could go across on dry land. When the Egyptian army followed, the water rushed back and destroyed them. No wonder Moses and the Israelites sang to the Lord! *Read Exodus 15:1-18.*

1. Although we don't know the tune, this is a song that Moses and the Israelites sang after God's victory at the Red Sea. As you read the words, where do you "hear" the singers' voices change to grow louder? softer? harsher? sweeter? slower? faster? more contemplative? more joyful?

2. Imagine that you are the last Israelite to make it across on dry land. You scramble onto the farther shore of the Red Sea, grab a couple of deep breaths, then turn around to see how close Pharaoh's chariots are following you. All you see is a churning body of water. People around you start to sing and dance. What do you feel? What do you do?

3. From a human standpoint, why did the Israelites and the Egyptians seem unevenly matched, with Israel sure to lose (vv. 1-5)?

4. Why did the Lord fight against the Egyptians (vv. 6-10)?

5. What was Israel's role in this victory?

6. How does God's power compare with the power of other "gods" (vv. 11-12)?

7. The people who sang this song had been powerless slaves through all their living memory. They had also lived surrounded by the gods of the Egyptians. No doubt many of them had come to think of the Hebrew God as an old legend peculiar to Israel. What would this dramatic experience have taught them about the Lord?

8. Because of God's victory at the Red Sea, how did Israel view the future (vv. 13-18)?

9. Think of a situation in which you were sure you were defeated and God won the battle for you. How do you know it was God?

10. How have God's victories given you hope for your future and the future of people you care about?

11. If the Lord is a warrior, how can we make sure we are on his side and not against him?

12. What spiritual battles do you now face?

13. What steps will you take this week to ensure that you stay on the Lord's side in your battles?

Praise God for how he fights your battles for you. Thank him for past victories, and thank him in advance for victories he is going to win. Pray that you will live in expectation of his victory.

Now or Later

• Study David's victory over Goliath (1 Samuel 17) with special attention to David's words in verses 45-47.

• Study Jehoshaphat's victory over the invading armies (2 Chronicles 20) with special attention to Jehoshaphat's prayer in verses 5-12 and Jahaziel the prophet's words in verses 15-17.

Suggested hymns to read or sing
Who Is on the Lord's Side?
Soldiers of Christ, Arise
Onward, Christian Soldiers
Stand Up, Stand Up for Jesus

3

Peacemaker

We can be sure that no matter when you are reading this, war is going on somewhere in the world. Does that sound pessimistic? Given the history of the human race, it is realistic. "Blessed are the peacemakers," Jesus said (Matthew 5:9). Gideon built an altar and named it "The LORD is Peace" (Judges 6:24). Yet in the previous study we saw that God is called a Warrior. How can he also be a Peacemaker?

GROUP DISCUSSION. In what sense is "peace" more than simply the absence of conflict?

PERSONAL REFLECTION. Who has acted as a peacemaker for you, and how?

Because they consistently rebelled against the Lord and worshiped idols, Jerusalem was conquered, and the people were exiled to Babylon in 597 B.C. A hundred years earlier, Isaiah wrote prophetically about this traumatic time in Hebrew history. In the passage we will read, God himself speaks, giving reasons for the exile and extending his promise that the people will return from Babylon. *Read Isaiah 48:16-22.*

1. What promises and conditions does God put forth for his people in this passage?

2. Why is peace so difficult to achieve between people? within ourselves?

---

3. In verse 16 God is called the "Sovereign LORD." How does God's sovereignty enable him to be a peacemaker?

---

4. What would have brought about peace for the people, along with other benefits (vv. 17-19)?

---

5. Suppose you heard the Lord (through the prophet) speak verses 17-19 to you, including those heartbreaking words "if only" (v. 18). Would you still find hope in what God said? Why or why not?

---

6. When has obedience to God's commands brought you peace (v. 18)?

---

7. In what ways does peace resemble a river (v. 18)?

---

8. The mood of the passage changes abruptly at verse 20. Although verses 20-21 do not specifically refer to peace, what is peaceful about the picture they portray?

9. What is the relationship between peace and hope?

10. What are some conflicts experienced by "the wicked"—those in rebellion against God (v. 22)?

11. Where do you need the Lord to act as a peacemaker? (Between himself and you? Between you and another person? Within yourself?)

Pray about conflicts you are facing. Pray for peace in your larger community, in your fellowship and throughout the world.

Now or Later

- Study Colossians 1:21-23, concerning how Christ reconciles us to God and transforms us from God's enemies into his friends.

- Study James 4:1-10, in which James takes on the question of what causes people to fight.

- Discuss or write about this question: What is the difference between making peace and knuckling under to a bully?

- How can you act as a peacemaker this week?

Suggested hymns to read or sing
Like a River Glorious
Joys Are Flowing Like a River
Be Still, My Soul
It Is Well with My Soul
Dear Lord and Father of Mankind

4

Vineyard Owner

It's the third year for our blueberry bushes. We've pruned, fertilized, waited and watched, and finally we have harvested a few handfuls of berries. But today one of the three bushes looks shriveled. Dryness is not the problem; the other bushes are green. What's wrong? We feel concerned, and I admit we also feel cheated. We've invested time and care in that plant. Just when we expected a nice crop of fruit, is it going to die on us?

God lovingly tends his people, and he wants to see a kind of fruit that is more lasting than blueberries.

GROUP DISCUSSION. Talk about your answers to the following statement:

When I have invested time and energy in another person, I expect:
___ thanks
___ visible results in the person's life
___ recognition
___ nothing in return
___ a sense of accomplishment
___ a reward in heaven

___ a sign from God that I have done right

___something else:

PERSONAL REFLECTION. Over the years what kind of fruit has the Lord produced in your life because of your trust in him?

In both the Old and New Testaments, the people of God are pictured as his vineyard. He plants, tends and cares for the vines (in this role we might call him a "Vinedresser"). Naturally, he expects a harvest. *Read Isaiah 5:1-7.*

1. What can you say about the relationship between God and his vineyard in this passage?

2. What do you think are some marks of a fruitful Christian life?

3. What efforts did the vineyard owner put forth for his vineyard (vv. 1-2)?

4. Why were the results disappointing (vv. 2-4)?

5. What are some examples of "bad fruit" in a believer's life?

6. How do you know that the vineyard itself is responsible for its own failure to produce fruit (that is, it cannot blame the vineyard owner)?

7. How do you respond to the way the vineyard owner treated his unfruitful vineyard (vv. 5-6)?

__ shocked

__ they deserved it

__ they should get another chance

__ some other response:

8. Verse 7 leaves no doubt about the identity of the vineyard and of the fruit God expected. What evidence do you see that the fruit God wants is not merely for our personal enjoyment?

9. What would you say justice and righteousness would look like in your community (v. 7)?

10. Consider two or three examples of good fruit that the Lord has produced or is producing in your life. What were some steps of the fruit-bearing process?

11. What "bad fruit" would you like God to prune out of your life?

12. How will you cooperate with the Lord this week to eliminate bad fruit and produce the good fruit of justice and righteousness?

Ask God for the courage to let him prune the vineyard of your life. Pray that you will always produce the fruit God longs to see.

Now or Later

* Study John 15:1-8, in which Jesus pictures himself as the true vine, with us as his branches and God the Father as the vinedresser.

* Study Luke 6:43-45 and Matthew 7:15-20, in which Jesus says that a person's character is revealed in the fruit of the person's life. (In Luke the application is more general, while in Matthew the focus is on false prophets.)

* Study Psalm 80:8-19, another Scripture passage that represents Israel as a vine planted by God.

* If some members of your group have a garden or fruit trees, discuss how you feel about unproductive plantings and how you deal with them. Draw comparisons with Isaiah 5:1-7.

* In commentaries or Bible reference books, read more about vineyards in Israel.

Suggested hymns to read or sing
We Give Thee But Thine Own
Take My Life and Let It Be

5

Builder

All the treehouses I have ever seen looked cockeyed. They displayed odd angles and appeared to be cobbled together from scraps of wood, which they probably were. Such haphazard construction is acceptable in a treehouse; we would be shocked to see it in a house going up in a new subdivision. We expect professional builders to show professional craftsmanship.

God the Creator is the ultimate master craftsman. When he put the universe together, he did it right and he did it well.

GROUP DISCUSSION. What is the most complicated thing you have ever built (or tried to build)? How did it turn out, and how did you feel about your work?

PERSONAL REFLECTION. Take time to quietly observe some part of the natural world, large or small. Make notes about how it reveals God's creative power and skill.

Afflicted with every kind of trouble, Job complained to God and asserted his own innocence. While Job's friends talked and talked, God remained silent. At last God spoke, not to directly answer Job's questions but to compare Job's puny knowledge with his own ultimate wisdom. *Read Job 38:1-18.* (God's answer to Job continues through 41:34.)

1. Count the questions that God asks Job in this passage. What do they have in common?

2. God broke his silence in response to Job's accusations of his unfairness. Yet God does not mention the issue of fairness. What does God communicate through his questions?

3. To what human activity does God compare his creation of the earth (vv. 4-7)?

4. Based on verses 4-7 what qualities would you expect to observe in the created world?

5. Why is the image of a barred door appropriate for the sea (vv. 8-11)?

6. In verses 12-18 other images are brought in besides that of a master builder. How does each reinforce the idea that God is all-wise and has made everything?

7. If God wanted to remind Job that he is the Creator, he could have repeated the creation story told in Genesis 1. How is God's challenge to Job strengthened because it comes in the form of questions?

8. How would you sum up God's message to Job in one sentence?

9. How does the image of God as a master builder encourage you to trust him?

10. Where does the world seem *not* to have been made by a master builder?

11. Where does your own life seem not to have been made by a master builder?

12. Reread your statement from question 8. How well does it apply to you?

13. As a result of this study, what new thing would you like God to build in your own life? Take into account both attitudes and actions.

Consider that without God there would be nothing: no stars, mountains, forests, animals, sunsets, and certainly no people to enjoy them. Pray that you will be more aware of the beauty and worth of all God has made.

Now or Later

* Draw a "comic strip" series of pictures to illustrate Job 38:4-18, portraying one Scripture passage per panel:

  vv. 4-7

  vv. 8-11

  vv. 12-13

  vv. 14-15

  vv. 16-18

* Read the rest of God's answer to Job in 38:19—41:34. Discuss how it modifies or adds to the image of God as builder.

* Reflect on John 1:1-3, which tells us that Christ, the *Logos* or Word, was involved in every aspect of the creation of the world. How does that idea expand your ideas of Jesus Christ?

* Study Ephesians 2:19-22 and 1 Peter 2:4-8, two New Testament passages that use the metaphor of the Lord as the builder—with us as the building!

Suggested hymns to read or sing
I Sing the Mighty Power of God
The Spacious Firmament on High
For the Beauty of the Earth
All Creatures of Our God and King
O Master Workman of the Race

6

King

Steeped in modern democracy, we find it hard to imagine life under a monarchy. Think of an absolute ruler and our minds are filled with words such as *dictator, despot, tyrant, strong man.* We like kings and queens only when they are ceremonial rulers, upholding a national tradition but lacking real political power.

The Bible insists that God is King. He cannot be voted out. What do we do with this picture of God as King? Is it only archaic language? And if he is truly *the* King, then what is our position, we who are not accustomed to standing in awe of anyone?

GROUP DISCUSSION. If you ran the world, what is one thing you would *not* change?

PERSONAL REFLECTION. What person have you held in awe? Has your opinion of that person ever lessened, and if so, why?

Many psalms and other passages of Scripture celebrate the Lord as King. We have chosen only one example. *Read Psalm 99.*

1. In what ways is this King superior to any earthly ruler?

2. What sort of reactions do you think this psalm is meant to inspire in the reader or hearer? How well does it succeed with you?

3. Because the Lord reigns, the nations should tremble and the earth should shake (v. 1). Yet only two psalms earlier we read "The LORD reigns, let the earth be glad; let the distant shores rejoice" (Psalm 97:1). How do you reconcile these two statements?

4. How should other nations relate to the Lord, God of Israel, and why (vv. 2-3)?

5. Why are verses 1-3 good news for the nations?

6. What qualities of the King does the psalmist single out in verses 4-5?

7. The nations around Israel feared their gods and had to appease them with rituals and offerings. In that context what is revolutionary about verses 6-8?

8. When we pray, we are speaking with the King of the universe. How should that awareness change our prayers (if it should)?

9. Verse 8 serves as a snapshot of how God deals with sin. What does it reveal about God's character?

10. To whom do you think the psalmist addressed verse 9?

11. Consider a time you became intensely aware that you were in the King's presence. Did the realization come suddenly? gradually? How did it affect you?

12. How can you change your habits or attitudes in prayer to be more aware that you are in the presence of the King?

The Lord, the King, is holy (vv. 3, 5, 9). Spend time in silence before the King of the universe. Honor him with words or songs, or simply listen to him and be in awe.

Now or Later

- Study other psalms about God the King, for example Psalms 24 and 47.
- In your own words, paraphrase 1 Timothy 1:17.

Suggested hymns to read or sing
Rejoice, the Lord Is King
Praise, My Soul, the King of Heaven
O Worship the King, All Glorious Above
Let All the World in Every Corner Sing
Crown Him with Many Crowns

7

Father

Say the word *father* to a group of people, and you set up unpredictable waves of emotions. Many fathers lead their children with wise discipline and loving care. At the other extreme, some fathers walk away from their children even before birth. Many adults wish they had been closer to their fathers. Others are glad they have always been close or have cultivated that closeness later in life. We can be sure of one thing: every father in the crowd will wish he had done a better job. Then we hear that God is our perfect heavenly Father. Certainly that does not mean he indulges our every demand or lets us get away with everything. Then what does it mean for us to call God *Father?*

GROUP DISCUSSION. Most fathers feel they could be doing, or could have done, a better job. Why do you think their doubts are so common?

PERSONAL REFLECTION. How do you think fatherly love differs from motherly love (if it does)?

Hosea was a prophet of the eighth century B.C. Assyria would soon conquer the Northern Kingdom of Israel with its capital in Samaria. Most of the book of Hosea portrays God as the patient and redeeming husband of an unfaithful wife. In chapter 11, however, a different image of God emerges: God as father of Israel. *Read Hosea 11:1-11.*

1. What conflicting emotions of God's are revealed in this passage?

2. Consider how God's heart is deeply hurt by the rebellious behavior of his children. In what ways is this a new thought to you? If it is not a new thought, how have you been aware of it before?

3. What had God done for Israel (vv. 1-4)?

4. How has God taught, led and fed you? Think of specific examples.

5. Despite God's faithfulness and care, how did Israel show ingratitude toward him (v. 2)?

6. What did God propose to do as punishment (vv. 5-7)?

7. What characteristics of a father's heart burst through in verses 8-9?

8. How does God the Father differ from even the best human father (v. 9)?

9. As a result of God's mercy, what will happen to his children (vv. 10-11)?

10. Israel hurt God's heart through rebellion and idolatry. The heart of God has not changed. Where might you be hurting him through areas of idolatry, that is, making anything but God supreme in your life?

11. What would you like to say to your heavenly Father about any areas of rebellion against him?

12. How would you like to thank him for being a faithful Father to you?

13. What definite steps will you take to become a more grateful and obedient child of your heavenly Father?

Thank your Father in heaven for teaching, feeding and leading you.

Now or Later

- Study John 1:10-13, which tells us how we become the children of God through faith in Christ.

- Study Psalm 103, especially verses 8-18, a beautiful picture of God's fatherly compassion toward us.

- We cannot say the Lord's Prayer without calling God "Our Father." Jesus responded with this prayer when his disciples asked him to teach them to pray (Luke 11:1-4; see also Matthew 6:9-13). Discuss why you think Jesus began his model prayer by addressing God as "Father" rather than some other name such as "Lord" or "Master," even though they would also be appropriate.

- No matter what time of year it is, make a Father's Day card for the Lord.

Suggested hymns to read or sing
Dear Lord and Father of Mankind
This Is My Father's World
O My Soul, Bless Thou Jehovah
Father, I Stretch My Hands to Thee
Great Is Thy Faithfulness
Any musical setting of The Lord's Prayer

8

Husband

The search for a life partner is one of humanity's strongest and most basic drives. Much of our society is organized around it. The movement of the two sexes toward each other fuels all sorts of industries, from flowers and bridal gowns to popular music and romantic movies.

In the context of that most promising and testing of human connections, God dares to call himself our Husband. Here there is no room for those tired old "marriage" jokes. This is a flawless Husband, and he is willingly wedded to a very flawed bride.

GROUP DISCUSSION. What makes marriage unique among all other human relationships?

PERSONAL REFLECTION. What three shortcomings in a wife would most severely test a husband's love?

The prophet Isaiah foresaw a time when the Jewish people would go into exile because of their idolatry and rebellion against the Lord. He also saw beyond that time, that after a period of hardship, God would have mercy, and the people would return. *Read Isaiah 54:1-8.*

1. What qualities of an excellent husband does God display?

2. Through the prophet Isaiah, God addresses a "barren woman" (v. 1). The context shows us that the words are addressed to the people of Israel rather than to one particular woman. In what ways could an entire nation be considered barren?

3. When have you experienced something like spiritual barrenness?

4. In Isaiah's time, a husband could divorce his wife if she failed to bear children. In light of that fact, what is remarkable about the promises that God, as Israel's husband, makes to Israel in verses 1-4?

5. Think of a time you felt ashamed or humiliated by your shortcomings. How did the Lord reassure you of his love?

6. Besides *husband*, God refers to himself by five different names in verse 5: Maker, Lord Almighty, Holy One of Israel, Redeemer and God of all the earth. How do these names enlarge the image of God as Israel's husband?

7. Israel had repeatedly abandoned God for the false gods of the nations around her. For this reason God would allow Israel to be taken captive into Babylon, but their captivity would not be the end of the story. What qualities of the heavenly Husband show through in the promises of verses 6-8?

8. In what areas of your life have you been unfaithful to the Lord and long for him to "call you back" (v. 6) or "bring you back" (v. 7)?

9. What would it look like for God to "bring you back" to himself? Think of practical consequences for yourself and others.

10. God promised "deep compassion" and "everlasting kindness" toward Israel (vv. 7-8). His kindness and compassion extend to us as well. How will you respond to his invitation to return?

11. How will you extend God's compassion and kindness to someone else this week?

The love of God is greater and more forgiving than the love of even the most compassionate human husband. Thank God for his love. Commit yourself to love him and remain faithful to him.

Now or Later

• Study Hosea 1—3, in which God portrays himself as a patient and redeeming husband to Israel.

• Study Revelation 19:6-10 and 21:1-13 concerning the coming marriage of Christ to his bride, the church, after his return.

Suggested hymns to read or sing
The Church's One Foundation
Still, Still with Thee
Jesus, Lover of My Soul
I Need Thee Every Hour

9

Potter

The vase didn't look like much. It was dark green and shaped vaguely like a cabbage. But it had been in my grandmother's house the whole time I was growing up, then later it was in the kitchen in my parents' home. When I sold most of my mother's antique vases and planters, I kept that pottery cabbage. It had lasted probably a century. I planted it with philodendron and set it on a pedestal on our glassed-in back porch.

Then came the night that raccoons invaded the porch. The next morning the green pot was a pile of smashed pieces that I could only sweep up and sadly discard.

What good is a broken pot? It no longer fulfills the intention of the potter. Through the prophet Jeremiah, God used the image of a potter to speak to a culture where clay pots were familiar everyday objects.

GROUP DISCUSSION. Take a ceramic pot of any kind, and call out or write down every possible use you can think for it. Then consider what flaws would make the pot unusable for each of those purposes.

PERSONAL REFLECTION. Have you ever wished you could remake your life? In what ways, and why?

Jeremiah prophesied in menacing times when Jerusalem was under threat of siege and conquest by Babylon. Despite their persistent idolatry, the people clung to the false hope that because God's temple was there, God would never let Jerusalem fall. *Read Jeremiah 18:1-12.*

1. How do the potter and the clay symbolize the workings of God with his people?

2. Imagine you are Jeremiah. In obedience to God's prompting, you go to a potter's workshop and watch him work, as described in verses 1-4. What sort of message do you expect God to reveal to you through what you have seen?

3. What are the two possible futures for the Jewish nation and, in fact, for any nation or kingdom (vv. 5-10)?

4. What would make the difference in the outcome for the nations (vv. 5-10)?

5. How do verses 11-12 demonstrate the mercy of God?

6. Suppose someone said, "This Scripture proves that people are help-less pawns, powerless in God's hands." How would you respond? Use specific evidence from the passage itself.

---

7. In God's hands what kind of "clay" do you tend to be?
__ brittle   __ like dry sand
__ pretty gritty   __ Silly Putty
__ usually pliable   __ Play-Dough
__ like cement after it's hardened   __ some other kind:
__ like wet sand

---

8. Notice that the potter did not smash the pot and throw it away, but reshaped it into something new. When your life was not turning out as God desired, what circumstances or people has God used to reshape you?

---

9. Through Jeremiah, God graciously warned the people to change their ways and avoid disaster (v. 11). Who might need a gracious warning from God through you?

---

10. What steps might you take, and what might you do and say, to warn that person who is in danger? (Before you rush to intervene, it is wise to make sure that you are the one God has picked for the job and that the timing is right.)

11. Where do you sense God trying to remold you?

12. What steps will you take to yield to the master Potter's design?

Yield up your life to God to let him shape you as he will. Thank him that he cares enough to bring change and renewal into your life.

Now or Later

- Study Isaiah 64:8-12, a prayer from the clay to the potter. The familiar words of the hymn "Have Thine Own Way, Lord" are derived from this passage rather than from Jeremiah 18. Two other references to potter and clay in Isaiah are 29:16 and 45:9; in both, the clay speaks defiantly against the potter.

- Study Romans 12:1-2, where Paul urges us to let ourselves be shaped by God's will and not by conformity to the world. In Romans 9:19-21 Paul uses the image of potter and clay specifically in reference to God's sovereign choice of the Jewish people.

- If possible, visit a studio where artisans make clay pots, preferably on a wheel. Talk with a potter about the qualities of good workable clay and the process of shaping a pot, and especially how a pot that goes wrong is reshaped. If you visit a school, take note of differences in the approaches of a master potter and of students just learning the craft.

Suggested hymns to read or sing
Have Thine Own Way, Lord
Take My Life and Let It Be
Make Me a Captive, Lord
Lord, Speak to Me, That I May Speak

10

Judge

Psalm 7

One of the best actors in our community theater group was the judge of our circuit court. He was especially convincing when he played shifty criminal types. One day I asked him how he got to the heart of those shady characters so well, since he stayed on the right side of the law himself. He answered, "Those are the kind of people I deal with all the time." Of course! Who understands lawlessness better than a person whose job it is to enforce the law?

Nobody understands our corrupt hearts better than our holy God, whose character is the exact opposite of sin. Though he understands us through and through, he never condones our rebellion.

GROUP DISCUSSION. If you were asked to judge a dispute, how would you respond?

____ I would enjoy the process of uncovering who was right and who was wrong.

____ I would want to act as a peacemaker and avoid the issue of who was in the wrong.

____ I would doubt my ability to find out the truth.

____ I would be too wishy-washy.

____ I would be glad for the chance to see justice done.

____ Some other response:

PERSONAL REFLECTION. When have you been a victim of injustice? What did you think and feel? If justice was finally achieved, how did it happen? If it wasn't, how have you dealt with it?

As we saw in study 1, we do not always know the circumstances that gave rise to David's psalms. In the case of Psalm 7, we know that David was threatened in some way by "Cush, a Benjamite," although there is no record of the conflict in any of the biblical accounts of David. As happened so often in David's life, danger led directly to prayer. *Read Psalm 7.*

1. Although David was threatened by enemies, his mood in this psalm is not cowering but confident. Why is he able to face opposition with such a bold spirit?

2. If David said this prayer on his feet, what postures do you see him taking throughout the psalm?

3. The word *judge* (as a verb) does not appear in the psalm until verse 8, and God is not identified as a *judge* (noun) until verse 11. How do verses 1-7 lay the groundwork for the idea of God as Judge?

4. Most of us would be nervous about appearing before a judge. How does David feel about the judgment of God (see especially vv. 6-9, 11)?

5. How would you respond to someone who said that David approached God with a self-righteous spirit, especially in verses 3-5 and 8?

6. What events have led you to pray something similar to verse 9?

7. What action will the Judge take against evil (vv. 10-13)?

8. How do wrongdoers bring judgment on themselves (vv. 14-16)?

9. What different perspective does verse 17 give to David's plea of innocence before the Judge?

10. What are some injustices that you would like to see the Judge put right?

11. Where might you be unfairly accusing others?

12. What will you do this week to bring justice, or at least to help tip the scales, in a situation close to home?

As you pray, surrender to the Lord, the Judge, every instance of injustice that troubles you. Resolve to trust him for the outcome. Thank the Lord for being all the things you have seen in this study guide, and more: Rock, Warrior, Peacemaker, Vineyard owner, Builder, King, Father, Husband, Potter and Judge.

Now or Later

• Expand on your answer to question 12. Draw a pair of scales (the scales of justice). On one side put words or pictures to symbolize the unfairness you see. On the other side put words or pictures to symbolize anything you can do to help put the situation right. As you prayerfully plan to take action, ask yourself: "Am I sure that I am the right person to take this action?" and "Is this the right time?" If God leads you to answer both questions "Yes," make definite plans to go ahead.

• Study Psalm 51, David's psalm of repentance after he committed adultery with Bathsheba. Although David does not address God as "Judge" in this psalm, he confesses that God has every right to judge him guilty, and he throws himself on God's mercy.

• Study 1 Peter 2:18-25, in which Peter urges anyone who suffers injustice to imitate Christ and put full trust in God, who judges justly.

Suggested hymns to read or sing:
There's a Wideness in God's Mercy
When Wilt Thou Save the People?
Lo! He Comes, with Clouds Descending
Hail to the Lord's Anointed

Leader's Notes

MY GRACE IS SUFFICIENT FOR YOU. (2 COR 12:9)

Leading a Bible discussion can be an enjoyable and rewarding experience. But it can also be *scary*—especially if you've never done it before. If this is your feeling, you're in good company. When God asked Moses to lead the Israelites out of Egypt, he replied, "O LORD, please send someone else to do it" (Ex 4:13). It was the same with Solomon, Jeremiah and Timothy, but God helped these people in spite of their weaknesses, and he will help you as well.

You don't need to be an expert on the Bible or a trained teacher to lead a Bible discussion. The idea behind these inductive studies is that the leader guides group members to discover for themselves what the Bible has to say. This method of learning will allow group members to remember much more of what is said than a lecture would.

These studies are designed to be led easily. As a matter of fact, the flow of questions through the passage from observation to interpretation to application is so natural that you may feel that the studies lead themselves. This study guide is also flexible. You can use it with a variety of groups— student, professional, neighborhood or church groups. Each study takes forty-five to sixty minutes in a group setting.

There are some important facts to know about group dynamics and encouraging discussion. The suggestions listed below should enable you to effectively and enjoyably fulfill your role as leader.

Preparing for the Study

1. Ask God to help you understand and apply the passage in your own life. Unless this happens, you will not be prepared to lead others. Pray too for the various members of the group. Ask God to open your hearts to the message of his Word and motivate you to action.

2. Read the introduction to the entire guide to get an overview of the entire book and the issues which will be explored.

3. As you begin each study, read and reread the assigned Bible passage to familiarize yourself with it.

4. This study guide is based on the New International Version of the Bible. It will help you and the group if you use this translation as the basis for your study and discussion.

5. Carefully work through each question in the study. Spend time in meditation and reflection as you consider how to respond.

6. Write your thoughts and responses in the space provided in the study guide. This will help you to express your understanding of the passage clearly.

7. It might help to have a Bible dictionary handy. Use it to look up any unfamiliar words, names or places. (For additional help on how to study a passage, see chapter five of *How to Lead a LifeGuide Bible Study*, InterVarsity Press.)

8. Consider how you can apply the Scripture to your life. Remember that the group will follow your lead in responding to the studies. They will not go any deeper than you do.

9. Once you have finished your own study of the passage, familiarize yourself with the leader's notes for the study you are leading. These are designed to help you in several ways. First, they tell you the purpose the study guide author had in mind when writing the study. Take time to think through how the study questions work together to accomplish that purpose. Second, the notes provide you with additional background information or suggestions on group dynamics for various questions. This information can be useful when people have difficulty understanding or answering a question. Third, the leader's notes can alert you to potential problems you may encounter during the study.

10. If you wish to remind yourself of anything mentioned in the leader's notes, make a note to yourself below that question in the study.

Leading the Study

1. Begin the study on time. Open with prayer, asking God to help the group to understand and apply the passage.

2. Be sure that everyone in your group has a study guide. Encourage the group to prepare beforehand for each discussion by reading the introduction to the guide and by working through the questions in the study.

3. At the beginning of your first time together, explain that these studies are meant to be discussions, not lectures. Encourage the members of the group to participate. However, do not put pressure on those who may be hesitant to speak during the first few sessions. You may want to suggest the following guidelines to your group.

☐ Stick to the topic being discussed.

☐ Your responses should be based on the verses which are the focus of the discussion and not on outside authorities such as commentaries or speakers.

☐ These studies focus on a particular passage of Scripture. Only rarely should you refer to other portions of the Bible. This allows for everyone to participate in in-depth study on equal ground.

☐ Anything said in the group is considered confidential and will not be discussed outside the group unless specific permission is given to do so.

☐ We will listen attentively to each other and provide time for each person present to talk.

☐ We will pray for each other.

4. Have a group member read the introduction at the beginning of the discussion.

5. Every session begins with a group discussion question. The question or activity is meant to be used before the passage is read. The question introduces the theme of the study and encourages group members to begin to open up. Encourage as many members as possible to participate, and be ready to get the discussion going with your own response.

This section is designed to reveal where our thoughts or feelings need to be transformed by Scripture. That is why it is especially important not to read the passage before the discussion question is asked. The passage will tend to color the honest reactions people would otherwise give because they are, of course, supposed to think the way the Bible does.

You may want to supplement the group discussion question with an icebreaker to help people to get comfortable. See the community section of *Small Group Idea Book* for more ideas.

You also might want to use the personal reflection question with your group. Either allow a time of silence for people to respond individually or discuss it together.

6. Have a group member (or members if the passage is long) read aloud the passage to be studied. Then give people several minutes to read the passage again silently so that they can take it all in.

7. Question 1 will generally be an overview question designed to briefly survey the passage. Encourage the group to look at the whole passage, but try to avoid getting sidetracked by questions or issues that will be addressed later in the study.

8. As you ask the questions, keep in mind that they are designed to be used just as they are written. You may simply read them aloud. Or you may prefer to express them in your own words.

There may be times when it is appropriate to deviate from the study guide.

For example, a question may have already been answered. If so, move on to the next question. Or someone may raise an important question not covered in the guide. Take time to discuss it, but try to keep the group from going off on tangents.

9. Avoid answering your own questions. If necessary, repeat or rephrase them until they are clearly understood. Or point out something you read in the leader's notes to clarify the context or meaning. An eager group quickly becomes passive and silent if they think the leader will do most of the talking.

10. Don't be afraid of silence. People may need time to think about the question before formulating their answers.

11. Don't be content with just one answer. Ask, "What do the rest of you think?" or "Anything else?" until several people have given answers to the question.

12. Acknowledge all contributions. Try to be affirming whenever possible. Never reject an answer. If it is clearly off-base, ask, "Which verse led you to that conclusion?" or again, "What do the rest of you think?"

13. Don't expect every answer to be addressed to you, even though this will probably happen at first. As group members become more at ease, they will begin to truly interact with each other. This is one sign of healthy discussion.

14. Don't be afraid of controversy. It can be very stimulating. If you don't resolve an issue completely, don't be frustrated. Move on and keep it in mind for later. A subsequent study may solve the problem.

15. Periodically summarize what the group has said about the passage. This helps to draw together the various ideas mentioned and gives continuity to the study. But don't preach.

16. At the end of the Bible discussion you may want to allow group members a time of quiet to work on an idea under "Now or Later." Then discuss what you experienced. Or you may want to encourage group members to work on these ideas between meetings. Give an opportunity during the session for people to talk about what they are learning.

17. Conclude your time together with conversational prayer, adapting the prayer suggestion at the end of the study to your group. Ask for God's help in following through on the commitments you've made.

18. End on time.

Many more suggestions and helps are found in *How to Lead a LifeGuide Bible Study.*

Components of Small Groups

A healthy small group should do more than study the Bible. There are four components to consider as you structure your time together.

Nurture. Small groups help us to grow in our knowledge and love of God. Bible study is the key to making this happen and is the foundation of your small group.

Community. Small groups are a great place to develop deep friendships with other Christians. Allow time for informal interaction before and after each study. Plan activities and games that will help you get to know each other. Spend time having fun together—going on a picnic or cooking dinner together.

Worship and prayer. Your study will be enhanced by spending time praising God together in prayer or song. Pray for each other's needs—and keep track of how God is answering prayer in your group. Ask God to help you to apply what you are learning in your study.

Outreach. Reaching out to others can be a practical way of applying what you are learning, and it will keep your group from becoming self-focused. Host a series of evangelistic discussions for your friends or neighbors. Clean up the yard of an elderly friend. Serve at a soup kitchen together, or spend a day working on a Habitat house.

Many more suggestions and helps in each of these areas are found in *Small Group Idea Book.* Information on building a small group can be found in *Small Group Leaders' Handbook* and *The Big Book on Small Groups* (both from Inter-Varsity Press). Reading through one of these books would be worth your time.

Study 1. Rock. Psalm 31:1-8.
Purpose: To continually take refuge in God for spiritual and physical protection.
Questions 1-2. "God often protected David physically, but when David and other OT writers call God their fortress, they primarily picture God as the unshakable strength of their souls, the source of hope and salvation that no enemy—physical or spiritual—can ever threaten. . . . Often rock and fortress are used together to refer to God (2 Sam 22:2; Ps 18:2; 31:3; 71:3). Fortified cities were built, if possible, high on a cliff or mountain, with the rock providing an unshakable foundation and impenetrable defense" (Leland Ryken, James C. Wilhoit, Tremper Longman III, eds., *Dictionary of Biblical Imagery* [Downers Grove, Ill.: InterVarsity Press, 1998], p. 305).
Question 3. As you explore the scriptural truth that God protects his people, group members are likely to raise questions (either aloud or silently) along these lines:

• Some of God's most faithful servants experience the most tragic circumstances. Why doesn't God protect them?

• If I take refuge in the Lord, will he protect me from accidents, illnesses and other misfortunes? If not, what good is the refuge God offers?

People do not raise such questions from intellectual curiosity but from disappointment, fear, confusion, even anger. Be sensitive to the feelings behind group members' questions. Admit that you have asked them yourself. As group leader, you should not flee from those questions, but neither should you feel obligated to furnish completely satisfactory answers. Don't let the discussion get sidetracked from the Scripture at hand; encourage group members to look for answers as you continue your study. The following ideas may help move your discussion along in a positive direction:

> Scripture, our own observations and our own experience teach us that God's people are subject to the same difficulties that a fallen creation brings on everyone else, and mature believers do not try to deny it. At the same time, everyone in your group will no doubt have a story of God's protection and deliverance from danger. Encourage group members to relate stories of the good that God has brought out of trouble and the ways he has clearly kept them from harm. Keep in mind that because of our human limitations, we do not know God's ultimate purposes for the things he brings into our lives (unless he specifically reveals his purposes to us).

Question 4. It will help to consider this question from both David's perspective and the Lord's perspective (as much as human limitations allow). David is interested in more than a safe place to hide; he is interested in knowing and trusting the Lord more deeply. And the consistent witness of Scripture is that the Lord wants to be more than a provider of good things for us; he wants to draw us into a trusting personal connection with himself. The most obvious human parallel is that of parents who want to be good providers but whose deeper desire is to build a relationship of love and trust with their children. In study seven you will more fully explore the scriptural image of God as Father.

Questions 7-8. If time allows, invite people to compare each undependable fortress with some inferior refuge they mentioned in their answers to question 6. For example, depending on money is like taking refuge on a beach because it can be swept away in the "rising tide" of inflation or a stock market crash.

Question 10. "[W]e see an interesting coincidence of language when moving from Luke 23:46 to the way in which both Matthew and John report Jesus' death. Luke, in the words of the psalm, reports that Jesus 'commits his spirit,' while Matthew 27:50 records that Jesus 'yielded up his spirit' and John 19:30 has it that Jesus 'delivered up his spirit.' Luke is the only writer who actually cites Psalm 31:5 here, but these parallels suggest the common use of a very old tradition rooted in the psalm" (Joel B. Green, Scot McKnight, I. Howard Marshall, eds., *Dictionary of Jesus and the Gospels* [Downers Grove, Ill.: InterVarsity Press, 1992], p. 151).

Question 13. As an alternative, ask: "Why would someone choose to face temptation directly rather than take shelter from it?" or "Where do you prefer to stand out in the open rather than taking shelter in the Lord?"

Study 2. Warrior. Exodus 15:1-18.

Purpose: To place ourselves firmly on the Lord's side in the battles he wages.

General note. The Israelites' miraculous crossing of the Red Sea is subject to much popular imagery from movies and cartoons—some accurate, some not. To prepare for this study, refresh your memory of the story of the exodus by reading at least Exodus 12:31—14:31 and preferably Exodus 3—14.

Questions 1-2. To capture an even stronger sense of the festive atmosphere on the shore, read Exodus 15:19-21, which says that Moses' sister Miriam and the other women played tambourines and danced while Miriam sang.

"As a fitting conclusion to the preceding account of the divine deliverance of the enslaved Israelites from Egyptian control, Moses and the people celebrated in song the majesty and power of 'the LORD' (1-18). Significantly, the narrative switches from prose to poetry. The exalted language of the poetry conveys better than prose the thoughts and feelings of the Israelites as they worshipped the one who had taken pity upon them and rescued them from the tyrant's power. By going over again what has already been recorded in prose, the reader too is encouraged to participate in the celebrations of the Israelites. As the people responded in adoration and praise for what God had already done, they looked forward with confidence to the future. Thus their song concludes by focusing on what God has yet to accomplish on their behalf (13-18). In the light of past events and future expectations it is hardly surprising that at the end of this section we read of Miriam and all the women playing tambourines and dancing with joy" (D. A. Carson, R. T. France, J. A. Motyer, G. J. Wenham, eds., *New Bible Commentary: 21st Century Edition* [Downers Grove, Ill.: InterVarsity Press, 1994], p. 104).

Question 3. The Israelites were apparently on foot; at most they had oxcarts and donkeys. The Egyptian army pursued them with horses and chariots (vv. 1, 4). Pharaoh had dispatched his top army officers (v. 4). No doubt the soldiers were armed to the best of Egypt's capability. From a military standpoint, the Israelites appeared to have made a fatal mistake.

Question 4. God was angry that the Egyptians opposed him in his purpose to free the Israelites (v. 7). To better understand God's anger with Pharaoh, it would help to review the story of Moses' attempts to negotiate the release of the Israelites in Exodus 5—11. Note that Pharaoh's intention was to recapture the Israelites so they could continue to work for him (Ex 14:5); however, from 15:9 it appears that the Egyptian army had decided to take vengeance on the Israelites and kill them all.

Question 5. We do not read of anything that Israel did, only what God did. We do know that they hurried across the seabed when it opened up (14:22, 29). Note that Moses even told them, "The Lord will fight for you; you need only to be still" (14:14).

On the specific phrase "The LORD is a warrior" (v. 3): "The book of Exodus has been developing the idea of Yahweh fighting for the Israelites against the Egyptians and their gods, so here the Lord is praised as a warrior. This is a concept that remains significant throughout the Old Testament and even into the New Testament. It is especially prominent in the books of Samuel, where the title 'Yahweh of the Armies' (Lord of Hosts) is common. Yahweh is the king and champion of the Israelites and will lead them forth victoriously in battle. Ancient mythologies often portrayed gods in battle, but these depictions generally concerned the harnessing and organizing of the cosmos. Both Marduk (Babylonian) and Baal (Canaanite) subdue the sea, which is personified in their divine foe (Tiamat and Yamm respectively). In contrast, this hymn recognizes how Yahweh harnessed the natural sea (not representing a supernatural being) to overcome his historical, human foes. Nevertheless, bringing secure order out of conflict, being proclaimed king and establishing a dwelling are common themes both here and in the ancient Near Eastern literatures concerning cosmic battle" (John H. Walton, Victor H. Matthews, Mark W. Chavalas, eds., *The IVP Bible Background Commentary: Old Testament* [Downers Grove, Ill.: InterVarsity Press, 2000], p. 90).

"Israel and the entire ancient Near East knew almost constant warfare. Armies were always on the move, either in the interest of expanding imperial territories or defending against foreign encroachment. A warrior was a powerful person, either dangerous or comforting depending on whether he was attacking or defending. The biblical writers recognized God's sovereignty over their history, and as they witnessed victory or defeat in warfare, they envisioned God's presence in martial categories" (*Dictionary of Biblical Imagery*, p. 211).

Question 6. "Not only were the gods [of Egypt] always present and always ready to intervene in life; Egypt had its own national gods to apply themselves to the various aspects of life, and particularly one resident god, the king of Egypt, whose divine function was to apply his powers to the advantage of his land. One might fairly say that, for the really important phases of life, the miraculous was more real to the ancient Egyptian than the natural" (J. A. Wilson, "Egypt," in *Interpreter's Dictionary of the Bible*, vol. 2, George A. Buttrick, ed. [Nashville: Abingdon, 1962], p. 56).

As a possible follow-up question, ask "How does God's power compare with some of the lesser things we depend on for security?"

Question 7. The Israelites discovered, immediately and dramatically, that God was real and not simply an old story. They also witnessed firsthand that God was more powerful than Egypt's Pharaoh, its army and even its gods. They saw evidence that God was *for* them in some way that he was not for Egypt; perhaps they speculated about the reasons why. After severe skepticism about Moses (14:11-12), they saw evidence that God had chosen Moses to be their leader; however, before long they would doubt him again (16:1-3).

Question 8. What God has already done (vv. 1-12) leads Israel into great confidence about what God will do in the future. They look forward to more victories and to eventual safety in their own land. Every sentence in verses 13-18 includes the future tense "will," and each statement about the future is a positive one for Israel (although negative for the nations they will meet on their journey to Canaan).

Study 3. Peacemaker. Isaiah 48:16-22.
Purpose: To allow the Lord to work peace in our situations of conflict.

Question 2. "Basically the OT word for peace, *shalom*, means 'completeness,' 'soundness,' 'well-being.'. . . It is used when one asks of or prays for the welfare of another (Gn. 43:27; Ex. 4:18; Jdg. 19:20), when one is in harmony or concord with another (Jos. 9:15; 1 Ki. 5:12), when one seeks the good of a city or country (Ps. 122:6; Je. 29:7). It may mean material prosperity (Ps. 73:3) or physical safety (Ps. 4:8). But also it may mean spiritual well-being. Such peace is the associate of righteousness and truth, but not of wickedness (Ps. 85:10; Is. 48:18, 22; 57:19-21)" (D. R. W. Wood, ed., *New Bible Dictionary*, 3rd ed. [Downers Grove, Ill.: InterVarsity Press, 1996], p. 890).

Question 3. When we are involved in conflict, typically we see only one side of the argument. Even if we stand outside the situation and see both sides, we are often powerless to change the combatants' minds. God in his sovereignty can work in the hearts of all the parties involved and can bring about a change of attitude in each one. He can also arrange circumstances to bring helpful influences into each person's life.

Note that the final sentence of verse 16 includes three personalities: "the Sovereign Lord," "me" and "his Spirit." "This verse [v. 16] ends with a startling change of speaker: no longer the Lord, as in vs 15-16a, but one *sent* by him, as the *Spirit* is also sent. It could be the prophet, but it is more meaningful if it anticipates the 'me' of 49:1; 50:4; 61:1; in other words, the Servant in whom Jesus was to see himself. It is a remarkable glimpse, from afar, of the Trinity" (*New Bible Commentary,* p. 659).

Question 5. The Lord's tone is yearning rather than scolding. He still promises to be the people's Redeemer and to teach and direct.

On the Lord as Redeemer (v. 17): "Redemption involves the release of people, animals, or property from bondage through outside help. Their social, physical, or spiritual weakness makes redemption necessary. Only someone strong or rich can effect it, so God plays a leading role in redemption" (T. Desmond Alexander and Brian S. Rosner, eds., *New Dictionary of Biblical Theology* [Downers Grove, Ill.: InterVarsity Press, 2000], p. 716).

Question 6. "[I]n the Bible peace is a key characteristic of God and a prominent concept. As in its ancient counterparts, the Bible's prominent meaning of peace is political. But the political meanings of peace are associated with emotional and physical meanings and numerous images from the military, agriculture and home. . . . If 'peace' is literally political negotiations, the Bible builds onto this image the larger truth of complete reconciliation, physical and emotional, between feuding parties. In the Bible genuine peace is always just and moral. God's 'covenant of peace' is made possible by obedient priests who prevent God's wrath (Num 25:12). Peace is seeking the well-being of others and of oneself. . . . Thus 'peacemaker' was a political position, an ambassador of peace—someone who ended wars, brought physical safety and health to people, sought people's well-being, and brought justice. Jesus is the Prince of Peace because Jesus makes Jew and Gentile one, breaking their dividing wall of hostility and reconciling them (Is 9:6; Eph 2:14-17)" (*Dictionary of Biblical Imagery,* pp. 632-33).

Question 7. The comparison is obvious if we think of a deep, wide, quietly flowing river. However, a river does more than make peaceful scenery; it brings life where there would otherwise be a desert. In the arid land of Israel, water is a constant concern. For people living in that dry environment, any river would symbolize peace, no matter how fast or slow it ran, because it meant the security of a dependable supply of water.

Question 9. Conflict, whether interpersonal or within ourselves, often feels as though it will never end. We are on the verge of a breakthrough and then a fresh battle breaks out. Peace allows us to redirect the energy which conflict has absorbed, and it opens up new possibilities which conflict has stifled.

Study 4. Vineyard Owner. Isaiah 5:1-7.
Purpose: To resolve to bear fruit that will please the Lord.
Question 1. "Grapes were among the basic staple products of the ancient Near East and therefore the care necessary for a vineyard was well known. In the rocky and hilly terrain of Israel special care had to be taken to preserve the soil and the moisture necessary to produce good fruit. As the rocks were cleared from the hillside, the stones were used to create terraces to level the ground. This would prevent water drainage and soil erosion. More stones were used to build huts and watchtowers that would be used to protect the crop when it neared harvest time. Constant hoeing between the rows of vine was necessary to prevent weeds from springing up and sapping off the water supply in the soil. Various irrigation techniques were used to assure sufficient groundwater. If the ground did not have adequate moisture or if the vines were not pruned back, the resulting crop would be small and sour. Finally, some of the stones were also used for winepresses and cisterns on the site so that the grapes could be processed without risking damage during transportation" (*IVP Bible Background Commentary: OT,* pp. 589-90).
Question 2. The "fruit of the Spirit" named in Galatians 5:22-23 will be helpful here, but do not let group members get away with simply quoting the list; encourage them to think of other qualities and more detailed aspects of the qualities in Galatians.
Question 3. The vineyard "is God's not only because God loves it, but because he painstakingly prepared the land and planted it. He also carefully protected it. In this way the parable describes God's election of Israel as a nation (Deut 7:7-11) and his providential care of it. As with any vineyard, the vinedresser does all this work with the expectation of a fruitful and bountiful harvest" (*Dictionary of Biblical Imagery,* p. 915).
Question 4. The disappointing harvest of "bad fruit" (v. 2) is also translated "wild grapes" (KJV and RSV), "worthless ones [grapes]" (NASB), "bitter grapes" (CEV) and that "every grape was sour" (TEV).
Question 5. As in question 2, the list of sins from Galatians 5:19-21 will be helpful, but do not let group members stop there.
Question 8. God expected to see justice and righteousness (v. 7). Those are unselfish qualities. We do not pursue them for our own enjoyment but in order to put them into action toward each other, often at great personal cost.
As a follow-up, ask "How does being caught up in our own enjoyment allow injustice and unrighteousness to continue, even if we do not cause them directly?"
Question 9. Modify this question to make it as broad or narrow as you wish:

What would justice and righteousness look like in your nation? city? neighborhood? church? some other arena of life?

Question 10. Keep the emphasis on how the Lord is working in your lives, and avoid any comparison of each other's spiritual progress. What sounds like a small victory may be gigantic to that person.

Study 5. Builder. Job 38:1-18.

Purpose: To cooperate with God in building our lives according to his plan.

Question 1. Here are the assumed one-word answers to God's questions:

v. 2: Job (rather than his friends—implied by 40:3-5)

v. 4: Nowhere

vv. 5-11: God

vv. 12-18: No

Question 2. God did not break his long silence in order to brag about his creative works but to remind Job how little he, Job, understood about the world and why things happen. Job cannot even comprehend any of the wonders that God sets forth here (and continues to set forth for several pages).

Question 3. "In addition to images of human building, the Bible posits a God who builds. He builds material things, first of all. In a day when the work of an architect and builder were not differentiated, God is portrayed as a master builder in his work of creation. God is a hands-on builder: 'My hand laid the foundation of the earth' (Is 48:13 RSV). The work of God in creation is described in terms of foundations and beams being laid (Ps 102:25; 104:3); of measurements being determined, a line being stretched, bases sunk and a cornerstone laid (Job 38:4-6); of upper chambers being built in the heavens (Amos 9:6). We also find concrete references to God's employing such devices or instruments as calipers and tape-measures, buckets and scales (Is 40:12; Jer 31:27; Job 26:10; 38:4-7). What is celebrated in all this imagery is God's careful planning in creation and the intricacy and permanence of what he created" (*Dictionary of Biblical Imagery*, p. 128).

Question 4. The work described is carefully planned and orderly, but it is not somber; it is cause for celebration. For a follow-up question, ask "How and where do we see those qualities in nature?"

Question 6. Concerning the seal-stamped clay in verse 14: "Stamp seals and cylinder seals were produced by engraving a pattern into clay or rock. . . . A stamp seal pressed into wet clay brings shape, contour, design and meaning to that which has had no distinct or distinguishable features. The light of sunrise likewise brings topographical features into sharp relief" (*IVP Bible Background Commentary: OT*, p. 509).

Question 8. Answers will vary, but the following quote will be helpful as you discuss them: "God's purpose is not to give Job lessons about nature and certainly not to dazzle him with signs of his power and intelligence (which Job has never for a minute doubted). It is rather to reconsider the mystery and complexity of the world that God has created. Job is meant to realize that the natural order is parallel to the moral order of the universe. Much of it is beyond human understanding, some of it seems hideous, futile, or fearsome, but all of it is the work of a wise God who has made the world the way it is for his own purposes" (*New Bible Commentary*, p. 480).

Question 10. Two comments may be helpful: First, we understand that even the inconvenient features of nature, such as wind and rain, have their vital purposes; perhaps even the extremes of nature, such as hurricanes and earthquakes, are necessary for some reason we do not understand. Second, we know that the natural world is not as God originally intended, because it suffers the effects of the curse of sin (Gen 3:17-19; Rom 8:19-21).

Study 6. King. Psalm 99.

Purpose: To surrender every part of our lives to the Lord, the King.

Question 1. No earthly ruler can claim to be "enthroned between the cherubim" (v. 1). Though many have tried, none has ruled over *all* the nations (v. 2). No earthly ruler can ever be holy in the way that God is holy (vv. 3, 5, 9). No human being could be capable of the perfect justice the psalmist attributes to God (v. 4). No human being deserves worship (vv. 5, 9). Besides those specifics, the mood of the entire psalm is one of adoration and submission, which no one but God could ever merit.

"There is scarcely a grander or more widespread image used in the Bible than king. Impressive in physical appearance, honored and respected by his people, the king was the dispenser of protection, justice and mercy and a symbol of power and authority" (*Dictionary of Biblical Imagery*, p. 476).

Concerning the cherubim (plural of cherub) (v. 1): "The OT does not describe the appearance and general nature of cherubim clearly. They were generally represented as winged creatures having feet and hands. . . . To what extent they were thought to be possessed of moral and ethical qualities is unknown. They were invariably in close association with God, and were accorded an elevated, ethereal position" (*New Bible Dictionary*, p. 183).

Concerning God's holiness (vv. 3, 5, 9): "Throughout Scripture, holiness is pre-eminently a characteristic of God himself. The terminology is used to signify that God is wholly other, distinct and separate from everything that he has made, and different from the gods of human imagination. As the Holy

One, he acts in judgment against human sin and its consequences. Remarkably, however, he also chooses to dwell amongst those whom he has redeemed" (*New Dictionary of Biblical Theology,* p. 544).

Questions 3-5. In the Old Testament the term "the nations" generally means "the Gentiles," that is, all people who are not part of God's chosen people, the Jews. God's plan was not for his people to imagine themselves as superior to other nations, but to display God's justice and his mercy to the world so that all nations would acknowledge him as Lord.

Question 6. "'[J]ustice' must be understood as being the same word as 'righteousness,' and seldom as denoting the specialized concept of 'fair play,' or legal equity, with which the term justice is presently associated. . . . Since life's highest standard is derived from the character of deity, 'justice,' from the time of Moses and onwards (*cf.* Dt. 32:4), comes to distinguish that which is God's will and those activities which result from it" (*New Bible Dictionary,* pp. 634-35).

Concerning the "footstool" of verse 5: "First of all, it must be recognized that the ark of the covenant was considered the footstool of God's invisible throne. . . . Second, the footstool must be understood to be an integral part of the throne, representing the closest accessibility to the king. Third, the imagery of the footstool has significance because it is used to express the king's subordination of his foes. . . . Finally, worshiping at the footstool is another way of expressing the reverence that is shown by prostrating oneself at the feet of God or king" (*IVP Bible Background Commentary: OT,* p. 548).

Question 7. Unlike the pagan gods, Israel's God welcomes intimate conversation with his followers. When the psalmist mentions Moses, Aaron and Samuel (v. 6) it is clear that these three are only examples of those who speak personally with God. Exodus 33:11 even says that "The LORD would speak to Moses face to face, as a man speaks with his friend." The implication is that the psalmists' readers can enjoy the same fellowship with God if they approach him in an attitude of worship.

Question 9. Take note of the two sides of God's character displayed in his forgiveness and punishment. Most of us tend to focus on either a loving God who overlooks sin or a vengeful God waiting to display his wrath.

Study 7. Father. Hosea 11:1-11.

Purpose: To trust and obey God our Father.

General note. Group members may raise the issue of whether "Father" is an image of God in the same category as "Warrior," "Builder," "Vinedresser" and the other images in this study guide. We can see that God is *like* those other things; but isn't "Father" actually *who* he is, one of the Persons of the Trinity

(Mt 28:19)? Certainly God is literally the father of Jesus Christ (Lk 1:30-35) and spiritual father for all believers (Jn 1:12-13). Yet in all this we are faced with the limitations of human understanding and human language. The reality of God is beyond us, and God must communicate who he is in human word pictures. He knows that we cannot call him "Father" without bringing up images and associations of earthly fathers.

Background note. For background on the time of Hosea, read 2 Chronicles 26:1—32:33 and 2 Kings 14:23-29.

Question 1. Certainly any parent—or anyone who has worked with or cared for children—can empathize with the jumble of emotions in this passage. God grieves over Israel's opposition, recalls the innocence of their early days, dreads the destruction to come if they do not change, weighs the punishment they deserve, yearns to show mercy, looks ahead to the time when they will make the right choices, plans good for them.

Question 3. Verses 1-4 set forth a condensed history of Israel. "Out of Egypt" (v. 1) is a reference to the exodus; in the New Testament this verse is applied to Christ (Mt 2:15). The Baals were pagan fertility gods worshiped by the Canaanites; after Israel entered Canaan, the appeal of the Baals was a constant temptation for Israel to fall into idolatry (for a dramatic example, see 1 Kings 18). Ephraim (the name of one of Joseph's sons) is another name for the Northern Kingdom of Israel, the ten tribes which split with the two southern tribes after the death of Solomon (1 Kings 12).

"There is no more passionate and moving expression of God's heart than this anywhere in the Bible. God speaks as the loving father of Israel, who called his son out of bondage in Egypt. At that time Israel was like a helpless child, a new nation facing the might of the Egyptian empire, wandering in the desert with no prospects of food or drink. God taught them to walk, either *taking them by the arms* or (as the RSV) *taking them in his arms*. He led them gently, guided them with *cords of human kindness, with ties of love*. If the metaphor of parent and child continues, then we should translate v. 4b as: 'I became for them as those who lift a child to their cheeks. And I reached out to feed him' " (*New Bible Commentary*, p. 775).

Questions 7-8. "The surprise in this passage is the fact that God is reluctant to give up on the northern ten tribes. While judgment had been exercised by God in the past (as in the destruction of the five cities of the plain—Sodom, Gomorrah, Admah, Zeboiim and Zobah), he definitely would not act with such fierceness here. The question is why. . . . The sudden shift in Hosea 11:8-9 signals new hope for Israel. The main reasons for the shift from a message of judgment to one of hope are to be found in two facts: (1) Israel would suffer a full punishment for disloyalty and would go into exile under the Assyrian conquest, and (2) the character of God, like the faces of a coin, has two sides: judgment and compassion. In the freedom of God, he chose to deal with Israel after its exile under his attribute of grace and compassion. God is not like any human being whose emotions swing back and forth arbitrarily and whose wrath might suddenly turn vindictive rather than be equitable. . . . Even though they deserved the fate of Admah and Zeboiim, he would bring them back home from captivity, just as he had promised the patriarchs in times past" (*Dictionary of Biblical Imagery,* pp. 324-25).

John Wesley wrote of verse 8: "Not that God is ever fluctuating or unresolved; but these are expressions after the manner of men, to shew what severity Israel had deserved, and yet how divine grace would be glorified in sparing them" (*John Wesley's Notes on the Whole Bible: The Old Testament,* Sage Digital Library [Albany, Ore.: Sage Software, 1996], p. 2254).

Question 10. To give group members more direction for this question, say something like this: "Think of things you depend on, especially things you may be depending on more than God."

Study 8. Husband. Isaiah 54:1-8.

Purpose: To resolve to remain faithful to the Lord, the Husband of his people.

General note. The picture of God as the divine Husband is a richly rewarding image not only for believers who are married but also for those who are single. Woman may find the image particularly encouraging. In the love of God, we find a secure place where we need fear no rejection or desertion. God's unconditional acceptance reassures us even when human relationships fail.

Question 1. "The most important husbandly image in the Bible is not human but divine, as God is portrayed as the husband of his redeemed, who metaphorically constitute his bride and wife. 'Your Maker is your husband,' Isaiah says regarding God (Is 54:5 RSV; see also Jer 31:32). Several strands make up the motif of God as husband.

"One is the image of *God as lover.* It begins with God's act of betrothal, as God declares regarding Israel, 'You were at the age for love; and I spread my skirt over you . . . yea, I plighted troth to you and entered into a covenant with you, says the Lord GOD, and you became mine' (Ezek 16:8). . . .

"A second image is that of *God as jilted husband,* the victim of a wife's adulterous unfaithfulness. The book of Hosea is the extended text on the subject, as Israel is portrayed as a faithless wife whom God reclaims. In graphic language Hosea portrays faithless Israel as a wife, decked with her rings and jewelry, going after her lovers (Hos 2:13). Throughout the OT prophetic books, in fact, idolatry is pictured as adultery (Ex 34:15-16; Lev 17:7; Jer 3:6). . . .

"God as husband reaches a third dimension when God is portrayed as the long-suffering and *faithful husband who restores a faithless wife*. Again the book of Hosea is the major text, as God's relationship to Israel is imaged in the marital history of Hosea and Gomer. Despite a momentary impulse to abandon his idolatrous wife, God calls her 'like a wife forsaken and grieved in spirit, like a wife of youth when she is cast off,' as God reclaims her 'with great compassion' (Is 54:6-7)" (*Dictionary of Biblical Imagery*, pp. 414-15).

Question 2. "Zion is seen here with the patriarchal image of the tent. As a mother who has been blessed with many children, Zion will need a spacious tent. The tents were made of hand-woven, three-feet-wide strips of dark goats' hair. When more family members needed to be accommodated, additional strips could be sown on. The cords that stretched from center poles to corner poles would have to be longer and the stakes made of stronger, thicker wood in order to hold the weight" (*IVP Bible Background Commentary: OT*, p. 634).

The apostle Paul quoted Isaiah 54:1 to illustrate the new covenant under Christ, contrasting the two mothers Hagar and Sarah (see Gal 4:27).

Question 4. "To be a wife without bearing children has always been regarded in the East, not only as a matter of regret, but as a reproach which could lead to divorce. . . . It was believed that the gift of children or the withholding of them indicated God's blessing or curse (Ex. 23:26; Dt. 7:14), as also did the barrenness or fruitfulness of the land (Ps. 107:33-34)" (*New Bible Dictionary*, p. 123).

"A woman who was unable to bear children in the ancient world was believed to be under the punishment of deity, incapable of serving the function for which she was married and therefore liable to be rejected and abandoned by her husband. The word translated 'youth' here refers to one who has not borne a child. Her shame is her barrenness. She is a widow because her husband has abandoned her (as most marriage contracts allowed) and therefore is the object of reproach with little hope of remarrying. She is thus stripped of short-term support by a husband and the support in her old age that could be expected from children" (*IVP Bible Background Commentary: OT*, p. 634).

Question 6. The additional names convey infinite strength along with the deepest care and concern. This God has qualities far beyond those of any ordinary fallible human husband.

Question 7. God did show mercy to Israel and bring his people back from Babylon after seventy years of captivity. It is also significant that this chapter of Isaiah comes immediately after chapter 53, the "suffering servant" chapter, which portrays the coming Messiah, Jesus, who will offer himself as the ultimate sacrifice for sin.

Study 9. Potter. Jeremiah 18:1-12.
Purpose: To allow the Lord to shape our character according to his will.
Question 1. "The potter's house, or workshop, needed to be near the clay sources and where water was available. It needed space for the potter's wheel, a space for treading, a kiln, a field for storing vessels and a dump for those discarded items. Once the pot was fired there was painting to be done. The typical hand-turned wheel was made of two pieces of stone. The upper stone had a cone-shaped protrusion on the bottom that fit into a corresponding recess in the top of the bottom stone and served as a pivot. . . . There were two kinds of potter's wheel, a slow or hand-turned wheel (or a tournette), and the fast or kick wheel, which was rotated by foot. The potter shaped the clay vessel by hand on the smaller revolving stone that was on top. The lower stone provided the momentum and quickened the turning. The potter rotated the lower disk with his foot. This created a centrifugal force on the clay, which was shaped by the potter's hands as he exerted force to shape it against its own force" (*IVP Bible Background Commentary: OT,* p. 655).

"Beginning as a pliable and impressionable substance (Job 38:14; Ps 40:2), clay provides an excellent image for human beings as the work of God's creative hand (Is 64:8; Jer 18:6; Job 10:9; 33:6). The potter collecting clay (or mortar) worked it into the proper consistency by treading it, perhaps in the pit where he dug it (Nahum 3:14). . . . The prophet warns of impending judgment, a trampling on rulers as a potter treads his clay, suggesting a treading in preparation for God's reforming and refashioning (Is 41:25). As the master potter, God has the unquestionably sovereign right to give each of his creations a specific shape and purpose according to his will (Is 29:16; 45:9; Rom 9:21)" (*Dictionary of Biblical Imagery,* p. 155).
Question 4. Group members may question how the Lord, who does not change, could ever "relent" (v. 8) or "reconsider" (v. 10). These thoughts will be helpful: "[U]nchangeableness must not be thought of as if it were some type of frozen immobility. God is not some impervious being who cannot respond when circumstances or individuals change. Rather, he is a living person, and as such he can and does change when the occasion demands it. He does not change in his character, person or plan. But he can and does respond to our changes" (Walter C. Kaiser Jr., Peter H. Davids, F. F. Bruce, Manfred T. Brauch, eds., *Hard Sayings of the Bible* [Downers Grove, Ill.: InterVarsity Press, 1996], p. 109).

Question 5. "The potter, displeased with the pot he is making makes another out of the same clay. The Lord then declares that, like the potter, he is free to revise his intentions for Judah (6). The principle is developed in vs 7-10 and applied to any nation. The crucial point, however (11), is that, even though the Lord has formed a plan to judge his people, there is still time for them to repent and avert the disaster" (*New Bible Commentary*, p. 686).

Study 10. Judge. Psalm 7.
Purpose: To trust in the justice and mercy of the Lord, the just Judge.

Question 1. David knew that his vindication lay not in the opinions of his enemies but in the justice of God. In spite of appearances, he remained sure that God would judge in his favor.

Question 3. David appeals to God to take his side against his enemies (vv. 1-2, 6-7) and sets forth the case for his own innocence (vv. 3-5). David takes it for granted that God has the authority and the right to decide for him and against his enemies.

"In Scripture, God is 'the Judge of all the earth' (Gn. 18:25), and his dealings with men are constantly described in forensic terms. God's Law is a complex of moral goals and standards by which his rational creatures should live. Righteousness, *i.e.* conformity with his law, is what he requires of his human creatures, and he shows his own righteousness as Judge in taking vengeance, *i.e.* inflicting punitive retribution ('wrath') on those who fall short of it (*cf.* Ps. 7:11, RV; Is. 5:16; 10:22; Acts 17:31; Rom. 2:5; 3:5f.). There is no hope for anyone if God's verdict goes against him" (*New Bible Dictionary*, p. 636).

Question 5. Not only in this psalm but in other psalms (for example Ps 17; 18; 26; 35), David asserts his own righteousness before God. How do we reconcile his attitude with the apostle Paul's statement that "all have sinned and fall short of the glory of God" (Rom 3:23)? We could say that David lived before the full revelation of Christ and never read Romans, but the observation that all people are sinners did not start with the New Testament (see 1 Kings 8:46). David himself wrote in another psalm that God looks down from heaven and fails to find even one person who does good (Ps 14:2-3), and David did not exempt himself from that judgment. In Psalm 7, David apparently pleads innocent to some *specific* charge of wrongdoing: "O Lord my God, if I have done *this*" (v. 3, italics added). David is saying, "I'm not perfect, but I don't deserve these accusations."

"In the poetry of the OT there do arise affirmations of self-righteousness by men like David ('Judge me according to my righteousness, and establish the just', Ps. 7:8-9, AV; *cf.* 18:20-24) or Job ('I am . . . just and blameless' Jb.

12:4; *cf.* 1:1), that might appear incongruous when considered in the light of their acknowledged iniquity. . . . The poets' aims, however, are either to exonerate themselves from particular crimes that enemies have laid to their charge (*cf.* Ps. 7:4) or to profess a genuine purity of purpose and single-hearted devotion to God (Ps. 17:1)" (*New Bible Dictionary*, p. 635).

Question 7. On the "shield" (v. 10): "The shield was an ancient Near Eastern warrior's primary defensive weapon. Having the right type of shield in battle could mean the difference between life and death. . . . The OT frequently calls God a shield when emphasizing his ability to protect his people. . . . The metaphor is especially prominent in Psalms. Like a shield, the Lord protects his people from hostile enemies. . . . This shieldlike protection is evidence of his faithfulness and enables his people to be confident, not afraid" (*Dictionary of Biblical Imagery,* p. 785).

On the "sword" (v. 12): "The sword was the most important weapon of warfare in the ancient Near East and in the Greco-Roman world. Ranging from sixteen inches to three feet in length, with one or both sides sharpened, this implement was used for thrusting and slashing opponents in armed conflict. . . . The sword also symbolizes divine judgment. The psalmist warns, 'If one does not repent, God will whet his sword' (Ps 7:12 NRSV). Scripture even speaks of God's judgment as 'the sword of the Lord' " (*Dictionary of Biblical Imagery,* p. 835).

On the "flaming arrows" (v. 13): "The Old Testament never uses the word for arrows to describe the flaming arrows used by human armies ('firebrands' of Prov 26:18). In Akkadian there are a few references to the use of flaming arrows that kings rain down on the enemy. These arrows were presumably dipped in a type of oil or pitch and set on fire. The arrows shot by Yahweh are usually considered to be bolts of lightning (see 2 Sam 22:15; Ps 77:17-18 for the two in parallel). Lightning would fit well with the concept of flaming arrows in that it is sometimes just called fire" (*IVP Bible Background Commentary: OT,* p. 519).

Question 8. Verse 15 is echoed in Proverbs 26:27: "If a man digs a pit, he will fall into it; if a man rolls a stone, it will roll back on him."

Question 9. In the end David must throw himself on God's righteousness, not his own, as the grounds for his vindication.

Dale and Sandy Larsen are freelance writers living in Rochester, Minnesota. Together they have written more than thirty books and Bible studies, including the LifeGuide® Bible Studies Images of Christ *and* Images of the Spirit.